ONE VOTE AWAY

A BRIEF HISTORY OF THE SUPREME COURT OF THE UNITED STATES

D0818538

Table of Contents

Introduction

We the People of the United States, in order to form a more perfect Union, establish Justice, insure domestic Tranquility, provide for the common defense, promote the general Welfare, and secure the Blessings of Liberty to ourselves and our Posterity, do ordain and establish this Constitution for the United States of America.

– The Preamble to the US Constitution

Following the American Revolutionary War, the United States of America had established itself as an independent nation, but the fledgling nation had many teething problems to deal with. Only a few years after the war ended in 1783, James Madison, George Washington, and Alexander Hamilton had good reason to believe their new country would implode. The Articles of Confederation, America's first constitution, gave the Confederation Congress the authority to create rules and request funding from the states, but with no power to enforce this authority, it was difficult to bring the states together as a united front. In addition, it had no power to regulate commerce or print money. With no ability to raise money in its own right, and being reliant on states to fund it, it was always doomed to failure.

With various states fighting over territory, taxation, and trade, the brand new country was on the brink of collapse, so Hamilton persuaded Congress to arrange a Grand Convention of state delegates to revise the Articles of Confederation to resolve the various problems.

The Constitutional Convention met in Philadelphia in May 1787. While the initial aim had been to revise the Articles of Confederation, it soon became apparent that a total overhaul of the existing governmental setup was needed. After months of debate and discussion, the new Constitution was signed on September 17, 1787. Thirty-eight delegates put their names to it, with George Reed signing on behalf of the absent John Dickinson of Delaware, for a total of 39 signatures.

The Constitution was significant on a number of levels. The creators all had concerns about centralizing power too much, since they were more interested in the interests of the state they represented. Their competing and sometimes conflicting opinions gave rise to a document filled with compromise - a document that has become one of the most long-lived constitutions in the world.

When it came to ratifying the Constitution, the founders decided to bypass state legislatures on the basis that members would be happy about ceding power to a national government. Instead, each state held special ratifying conventions. Nine of the thirteen states needed to ratify the Constitution to put the new government in place, but initially, only six states were pro-Constitution.

Once again, the country was divided, with the Federalists needing to convert three states to their side. Anti-Federalists strongly opposed the Constitution on the basis that it was establishing a powerful central government when they had just fought a war to break away from such a government. In addition, the absence of a bill of rights was another bone of contention. Federalists, meanwhile, believed a strong central government was necessary if the nation was to survive in the long term.

After a difficult, tense campaign, the Federalists finally won when the 'vote now, amend later' compromise swayed the remaining opponents, and the new Constitution was officially ratified. Delaware was the first state to ratify the Constitution on December 7, 1787. When New Hampshire ratified it on June 22, 1788, it was the ninth state to do so, meaning the Constitution had been approved.

The Confederation Congress was established on March 9, 1789, by which point all the states except Rhode Island and North Carolina had ratified the Constitution.

The Constitution had been written to establish a government that would have sufficient power to act on a national level but would not have so much authority that fundamental rights would be threatened. One way it did this was to separate the power of government into three branches, each with checks and balances on its powers, such that no one branch would be able to dominate the others. This reflected the negative experience the states had had with the King of England and Parliament. The Constitution clearly laid out the powers of each branch, with any remaining powers left in the hands of individual states.

In addition, a process was put in place to allow for amendments to the Constitution. It has been amended 27 times since its original ratification, although the process of change is quite onerous: an amendment needs to be proposed by a two-thirds vote of both Houses of Congress or, alternatively, by a convention called by two-thirds of the states. The amendment must subsequently be ratified by three quarters of the state legislatures or three-quarters of conventions called in each state for ratification. More recently, amendments have also come with a timeframe within which they must be ratified.

Article III of the Constitution described the court system of the newly independent country, including the Supreme Court. It detailed the types of cases the Supreme Court would take on as original jurisdiction, gave Congress the power to create lower courts, and established an appeals process. It also protected the right to trial by jury in criminal cases and set out the definition of what constituted treason.

Article III, Section 1, gave the judicial power of the United States to the federal courts, granting them the authority to interpret and apply the law in any given case, as well as the ability to punish, sentence, and resolve conflicts. The Judiciary Act of 1789 saw the Congress start to flesh out the details of the court system, and Title 28 of the US Code holds the full details of judicial powers and administration.

From the First Congress, Supreme Court justices would travel around to sit on panels to hear appeals from the district courts. This changed in 1891 when Congress put in place a new system giving district courts original jurisdiction. Circuit courts with exclusive jurisdiction would hear regional appeals before they went to the Supreme Court for consideration. However, the Supreme Court was given discretionary jurisdiction, which means that it does not have to hear every case brought to it.

Article III, Section 2, Clause 2, gave the Supreme Court original jurisdiction in cases involving ministers, consuls, ambassadors, and any foreign nation-states, as well as in cases that are subject to federal judicial power because at least one state is a party.

Although the Framers considered including it, no part of the Constitution gives express authorization to judicial review. The Constitution remains the supreme law of the land, although precedent has subsequently established that the courts can exercise judicial review over Congress or the executive branch. The Supreme Court was to decide Constitutional issues of state law on a case-by-case basis and only when absolutely necessary according to the Constitution, regardless of state legislators' motives, policies, or beliefs.

The Supreme Court held and continues to hold a pivotal role in the constitutional government of the United States. It is the highest court in the land, so it is the last chance for anyone needing to appeal in the pursuit of justice. Since it has the power of judicial review, it plays a crucial part in keeping each branch of government in check. It protects civil liberties and rights by quashing any laws which would violate the Constitution. Finally, it limits the power of democratic government by ensuring that laws cannot be passed which would harm minorities.

In short, the US Supreme Court's role is to uphold the fundamental values upon which the nation was founded: freedom of speech, freedom of religion, and due process of the law.

Chapter 1

Chief Justice John Marshall

John Marshall (September 24, 1755 – July 6, 1835) was the fourth Chief Justice of the United States Supreme Court. He held the position from 1801 to 1835, making him the longest-serving chief justice in Supreme Court history and one of the most influential justices to have served.

Before joining the Supreme Court, Marshall was the United States Secretary of State under President John Adams. One of the leading figures in the Federalist Party, Marshall had played a pivotal role in Virginia's ratification of the Constitution. Adams appointed him Secretary of State in 1800 before appointing him to the Supreme Court in 1801.

In the presidential election of 1800, the Democratic-Republicans were the winners, but the nominees, Thomas Jefferson and Aaron Burr, both had 73 electoral votes, meaning the Federalist-controlled House of Representatives had the responsibility of selecting a president. Hamilton asked Marshall to support Jefferson, but he refused to support either candidate.

Following a week of ballots, Jefferson was finally elected President, with Burr as his Vice President. Had the stalemate continued, Marshall would have become acting president due to his position as Secretary of State.

Following the election, Congress passed what was known as the Midnight Judges Act. This made a number of changes to the federal judiciary, most notably reducing the number of Supreme Court justices from six to five, meaning that Jefferson would not be able to appoint a new Supreme Court justice until two vacancies came up.

In late 1800, Chief Justice Oliver Ellsworth stepped down due to ill health. Adams nominated former Chief Justice John Jay to head up the Supreme Court, but Jay refused. With less than two months to go before Jefferson would take over as president, Marshall suggested to Adams that he should appoint Associate Justice William Paterson to Chief Justice, but instead, Adams told Marshall, "I believe I must nominate you."

While the Senate delayed confirming Marshall to the post, with many senators hoping an alternative candidate would be chosen, eventually Marshall was confirmed by the Senate on January 27, 1801, taking office on February 4. He continued to hold the position of Secretary of State until Adams' term as president ended on March 4.

Marshall soon made his mark on the court, partly due to his charismatic nature and influence on his fellow justices.

Before 1801, the Supreme Court was generally viewed as not being particularly significant. Most legal matters were resolved at the state level, and the Court had made only 63 decisions in the first few decades of its existence, few of which had had any significant impact. Moreover, it had never overturned any federal or state law.

Under Marshall, this would all change, and the Supreme Court would become a powerful force in the federal government. With Marshall at the helm, the Supreme Court issued over 1000 decisions, with roughly half of those being authored by Marshall himself. Despite the political domination of the Democratic-

Republicans, Marshall and the Supreme Court exerted a great deal of power on behalf of the federal government.

He led the Supreme Court away from delivering seriatim opinions on cases, where each Justice would give their opinion separately, instead preferring to issue a single majority opinion. Six months of the year, the justices were doing circuit duty across the various states. The Court would meet in Washington for two months, from the first Monday in February until the second or third week in March. During this time, the justices stayed together in the same boarding house, avoided socializing, and discussed each case together. They would come to a consensus quickly, usually within a few days.

Marshall had an ability to summarize the key aspects of a case and weave them together in a persuasive argument to bring other justices round to his way of thinking. By 1811, Democratic-Republican appointed Justices outnumbered the Federalists by 5-to-2, yet despite being the minority, Marshall was still very much in charge of the Court. It was rare for him to be on the losing side of a constitutional case. In fact, it only happened once in *Ogden v Saunders*. The case, heard in 1827, determined the parameters of a bankruptcy law as it related to a clause in the Constitution.

Marshall was a defining factor in shaping the Supreme Court, and his legacy persists today in the power the Court holds.

Chapter 2

Marbury v Madison, 1803

John Marshall wrote one of the most important cases in Supreme Court history: *Marbury v Madison*. It was the first US Supreme Court case to apply the principle of 'judicial review,' which was the power federal courts had to void acts of Congress they felt violated the United States Constitution. The case was instrumental in elevating the Supreme Court into a separate branch of government on an equal footing with Congress and the executive.

After the Democratic-Republican defeated the Federalists in the 1800 election, President Adams spent his last days in power appointing a large number of justices of the peace for the District of Columbia. Their commissions were approved by the Senate, signed by Adams, and affixed with the official government seal. However, the commissions were not delivered, so when Jefferson took office on March 5, 1801, he ordered James Madison, his Secretary of

State, not to deliver them. William Marbury, one of the appointees, denied his position as a consequence, petitioned the Supreme Court to compel Madison to show just cause for why he could not have his commission.

When deciding the case, Chief Justice Marshall considered three aspects: Did Marbury have a right to the writ he was petitioning for? Did United States law allow the courts to grant him said writ? If they were allowed, could the Supreme Court issue the writ?

Marshall ruled that Marbury had been properly appointed in accordance with the law, so was indeed entitled to the writ. Since he had a legal right to his commission, there would therefore be a legal remedy, and Marshall stated that it was the responsibility of the courts to protect the rights of individuals, even if this meant going against the decisions of the President of the United States. At the time, this statement was met with some controversy, since it was interpreted as criticizing and lecturing President Jefferson about the rule of law.

When it came to the question of whether the Supreme Court could issue the writ, Marshall's decision dealt with the issue of judicial review.

Chief Justice Marshall ruled that, although Marbury was entitled to the writ, the Court could not grant it because Section 13 of the Judiciary Act of 1789 was unconstitutional in cases of original jurisdiction. Original jurisdiction (the ability to take a case directly to the Supreme Court) was the only jurisdictional matter dealt with by the Constitution, and Article II stated that this only applied to cases involving "ambassadors, other public ministers and consuls" as well as those "in which the state shall be party." In extending the Court's original jurisdiction to cases such as Marbury's, Congress had overstepped the bounds of its authority. Marshall held that when an act of Congress is in conflict with the Constitution, the Supreme Court was obliged to uphold the Constitution, since, according to Article VI, it is the "supreme law of the land."

Consequently, Marbury was denied his commission. Although President Jefferson got the result he would have wanted, he was not happy about the way in which Marshall had delivered the verdict, since he did not appreciate being lectured, nor did he appreciate the fact that Marshall's decision reaffirmed the Supreme Court's ability to review acts of Congress.

Marshall was careful not to claim that the Court was the only authority that could interpret the Constitution, and he did not give any details about how the Court might enforce its decisions if they were opposed by Congress or the Executive. However, in asserting the principle of judicial review, Marshall laid the foundations for the establishment of the Supreme Court as a branch of government equal to the other two, and whenever the Court has needed precedence to affirm its legitimacy, it has always referred back to *Marbury v Madison*.

Chapter 3

McCulloch v Maryland, 1819

Another landmark case presided over by Chief
Justice John Marshall was *McCulloch v
Maryland*. In this case, the Supreme Court ruled
that the Necessary and Proper Clause of Article
I, Section 8 of the Constitution gave Congress
the ability to establish the Second Bank of the
United States. Moreover, the state of Maryland
had no legal right to tax the Bank.

This case was important because it gave
Congress the power it needed to move forward
with its plans for chartering the Second Bank of
the United States (BUS). In addition, it quashed
the radical states' arguments, which had been
presented by the counsel for Maryland, ending
their attempts to implement taxes on the
establishment.

At the heart of the case was the question of
whether the 1816 act of Congress establishing
the BUS was constitutional. While the Bank was

controlled by private stockholders, it held federal funds. On top of that, it had the power to issue legal tender in addition to the notes of individual states' banks. Since it held such a privileged position, the Bank agreed to lend money to the federal government instead of paying taxes.

Unsurprisingly, state banks viewed the BUS as a competitor and one which benefited from privileges they lacked. When the depression of 1818 hit, the state banks claimed that the BUS was to blame for their failing fortunes. As a consequence, the state of Maryland decided to tax 'any bank not chartered within the state.' It was no coincidence that there was only one bank that fit this criterion – the BUS. However, the Bank's Baltimore branch refused to pay the tax, so Maryland started legal proceedings against James McCulloch, the cashier of the branch. McCulloch countered that the tax was unconstitutional and took his case to the state court, which found in favor of Maryland. The court of appeals upheld the decision, so McCulloch took his case to the US Supreme Court.

In a unanimous decision that overturned the lower courts, the Supreme Court ruled that while the BUS was constitutional, the Maryland tax was unconstitutional. Citing the Necessary and Proper Clause of Article I, Section 8, the Supreme Court pointed out that this clause gave Congress the power to pass whatever laws necessary to execute its powers. These powers included the ability to regulate interstate commerce, collect taxes, and borrow money, therefore rendering the creation of the Bank perfectly legal and constitutional.

In comparison, Maryland could not tax the Bank because of the Supremacy Clause of Article VI of the Constitution, which stated that the laws of the United States would always hold sway over state laws in the event of a conflict. Marshall said that since "the power to tax is the power to destroy," Maryland was acting unconstitutionally by going against the federal laws and institutions of the United States.

Finally, the Court upheld the principle that the sovereignty of the United States ultimately lay with the people of the nation, not the individual states. It established that the United States was more than an alliance of states, but a nation of constitutional sovereignty with all authority emanating from the people who both created and were governed by the Constitution. Maryland's tax, therefore, broke constitutional law because it was, in effect, a levy against all the people of the United States by a state which was accountable to a small number of the people.

Where *Marbury v Madison* had shown that the Supreme Court could exert a great deal of power over the laws of the land, *McCulloch v Maryland* saw those powers put into practice. Indeed, there is a strong argument to say that this decision was the most representative of national power and what the Court could do.

With this decision, the Supreme Court laid down the principle that Congress' powers included ones laid down by the Constitution, both implicit and explicit, that the Union held a superior position over individual states, and that the federal government held constitutional sovereignty.

To this day, *McCulloch v Maryland* is one of the most important cases of American constitutional law.

Chapter 4

Gibbons v Ogden, 1824

Gibbons v Ogden saw the powers of Congress increase exponentially thanks to an interpretation of the Commerce Clause of Article I, Section 8. The Supreme Court ruled that the clause gave Congress the power to regulate any aspect of commerce which crossed state lines, which meant that this regulation trumped any existing conflicting state regulation. This case has subsequently granted Congress power over a wide array of national issues.

Gibbons v Ogden dealt with competing claims between rival steamship franchises. The state of New York had granted Aaron Ogden exclusive rights over steamboat ferry services on the Hudson River between New Jersey and New York City. However, another steamboat operator, Thomas Gibbons, was also running services along that route, so Ogden went to a New York state court to take out an injunction against Gibbons. He argued that the state had given him exclusive rights over that particular route and that Gibbons was acting illegally. Gibbons countered by arguing that a 1793 act of Congress gave him the right to operate.

The New York court found in favor of Ogden and ordered Gibbons to stop operating. Gibbons appealed, but the New York Supreme Court upheld the decision. Gibbons took his fight to the US Supreme Court, which agreed to review the case.

Upon examination, Chief Justice John Marshall ruled in favor of Gibbons, determining that New York's exclusive license to Ogden was a violation of the federal licensing act of 1793. This decision relied upon the first interpretation of the Commerce Clause of the US Constitution by the Supreme Court. The clause states that 'Congress shall have power to regulate commerce ... among the several States' and the Court determined that 'commerce' in this case did not just cover any articles being traded across state lines, but also navigation between the states.

In addition, the Court looked at the phrasing of the clause and decided that the word 'among' could be interpreted as 'intermingled with.'

Therefore, Congress's power to regulate commerce across state boundaries extended beyond boundary lines and into the interior of states.

This was key because it meant that Congress could pass any law regulating commerce as long as that commerce was carried out in more than one state. Therefore, Congress had the ability to regulate steamboat routes between New York and New Jersey.

The Court agreed with Gibbons that the licensing act of 1793 gave him the right to operate along the Hudson River, and the New York law was unconstitutional. The injunction against Gibbons was overturned and he was allowed to resume operations.

Gibbons v Ogden was important because it made it possible for the future expansion of congressional power over commercial activity and other activities previously held to fall under state jurisdiction. This was monumental because it meant that any state law regulating commercial activities - including laws governing working conditions - had the potential to be overturned by Congress if it could be demonstrated that the activity was involved in interstate commerce, which could mean something as simple as goods being sold across state lines.

Gibbons v Ogden laid the foundation for the subsequent rise of federal power into the 20th century.

Chapter 5

Dred Scott v Sandford, 1857

A controversial case, *Dred Scott v Sandford,* saw the Supreme Court rule that Americans who were of African descent were not American citizens, regardless of whether they were free or slaves. As such, they could not sue in federal court. The Court also ruled that Congress did not have the power to ban slavery in US territories and decided that the Fifth Amendment afforded constitutional protection to the rights of slaveowners since slaves were categorized as property.

The events leading up to the case began back in 1833, when Dr. John Emerson, a US Army surgeon, bought Dred Scott, a slave. He took Scott with him to a base in Wisconsin, where slavery was banned following the Missouri Compromise. Scott lived in the Wisconsin Territory for four years, before moving to Louisiana in 1840, taking with him his wife and children, then going on to St. Louis with Emerson.

Dr. Emerson died in 1843, and his wife, Eliza Irene Sanford, took ownership of his slaves. In 1846, Dred Scott tried to buy his family's freedom from her, but she refused, so he took her to court. Dred Scott argued that his family was free because they had lived in a territory where slavery had been banned.

In 1850, the courts agreed with Dred Scott and declared him a free man. However, his wages had been withheld during the hearing, and Mrs. Emerson had remarried, leaving her brother, John Sanford, in charge of dealing with the matter.

John Sanford did not want to pay the back wages Dred Scott was owed, so he appealed the court's decision. The Missouri Supreme Court overturned the ruling, so Dred Scott filed another suit. This time, he wanted to claim damages against John Sanford for alleged physical abuse. He took his claim to a federal circuit court, but the jury ruled he could not use the federal courts in this way because he was a slave under Missouri law. Scott went to the US Supreme Court, hoping they would overturn this decision.

Unfortunately for Dred Scott, the Supreme Court ruled that it did not have any jurisdiction in this case because Scott was a slave – or at least he had been a slave in the past.

There were a number of reasons for this decision. One was that federal courts could only hear cases brought by a very specific and limited number of parties. The Court ruled that, because Dred Scott was descended from slaves, this meant that he was not part of "the political community formed and brought into existence by the Constitution." In other words, he was not a citizen, so, therefore, could not file a lawsuit in a federal court.

Building on this decision, the Court determined that while Dred Scott might be a citizen of a free state, this did not automatically confer US citizenship on him. The Constitution gave Congress the sole authority to determine national citizenship, and since Scott was black, he could not qualify as an American citizen.

The final blow against Dred Scott was that, despite his living in the Wisconsin Territory, he could not be deemed free as a consequence because Congress did not have the power to ban slavery in US territories. Slaves were still legally viewed as property at that time, and the Fifth Amendment meant that Congress could not take away property from individuals without appropriate compensation. Although he had won his freedom, Dred Scott was not entitled to his wages.

The decision fueled existing tensions between the North and South. Those who were pro-slavery in the South took it as a signal to attempt to bring slavery back across the nation. In contrast, those who opposed slavery in the North were angered by the decision and there were violent outbreaks between slaveowners and abolitionists on the frontier.

After the Civil War, the Reconstruction Congress passed the Thirteenth, Fourteenth, and Fifteenth Amendments. Ratified by the states, these amendments overturned the Dred Scott decision, meaning that anyone born or naturalized in the United States was recognized as an American citizen, regardless of race, and may use the federal courts to settle appropriate matters.

Chapter 6

Plessy v Ferguson, 1896

Plessy v Ferguson saw the Supreme Court consider whether a Louisiana law was constitutional. Passed in 1890, the law required all passenger railways to provide separate cars for "white and colored races." The cars were to have equal facilities, and whites were not allowed to sit in black cars and vice versa, with an exception allowed for "nurses attending children of the other race." There were stiff penalties for any passengers or railway employees who broke the law.

Homer Plessy looked white but was one-eighth black. On June 7, 1892, he bought a first-class ticket from New Orleans to Covington and sat in a white-only car. He was arrested and subsequently convicted of breaking the 1890 law. Plessy filed a petition at the Supreme Court against the judge presiding over his trial, the Hon. John H. Ferguson, arguing that the law was unconstitutional since it went against the Equal

Protection Clause of the Fourteenth Amendment, which afforded "to any person within their jurisdiction the equal protection of the laws." In addition, the Thirteenth Amendment had banned slavery, something which Plessy argued also rendered the Louisiana law unconstitutional.

The Supreme Court ruled that while the Fourteenth Amendment gave equality of the races before the law, this did not extend to social rights, so railway cars could be legally segregated. The Thirteenth Amendment only concerned the imposition of slavery and not the treatment of those who were now free. The Court also held that since the railway cars provided equal facilities, with equal punishments for anyone who broke the law, there was no prejudice or attempt to treat blacks as being inferior. Anyone who believed that said law imposed a hierarchy between the races was simply choosing to interpret it in that way; the law as it stood did not actually do this.

One Justice made it clear that he disagreed with the decision. Justice John Marshall Harlan stated that "Our Constitution is color-blind, and neither knows nor tolerates classes among citizens." However, his lone voice was not enough to overturn the ruling, and segregation continued.

Until the middle of the twentieth century, *Plessy v Ferguson* was used to justify racial segregation in public places and, in many parts of the South, the black facilities in such places were markedly inferior to those provided for white people, fueling racial tensions and contributing to the creation of a two-tier society.

Chapter 7

Schenck v United States, 1919

Schenck v United States saw the Supreme Court create the 'clear and present danger' test to decide when the state had the right to limit someone's right to free speech as laid out in the First Amendment. It decided that there were occasions where words could present a 'clear and present danger' which Congress had the constitutional right to prevent.

Charles Schenck was a prominent socialist who had tried to disseminate thousands of flyers to American servicemen who had been called up to fight in World War I. Schenck's flyers claimed that the draft was tantamount to 'involuntary servitude' and therefore ran counter to the Thirteenth Amendment, which outlawed slavery. Moreover, the war was motivated by capitalist greed and thus was not something America should involve itself in, so Schenck tried to get support to repeal the draft.

As a consequence, Schenck was charged with breaking the newly enacted Espionage Act. The government claimed that Schenck had conspired to cause insubordination within the military and naval forces. Schenck countered that the Espionage Act violated the First Amendment, which prevented Congress from curtailing freedom of speech.

Schenck was found guilty, and he appealed. The US Supreme Court reviewed the case and upheld Schenck's conviction.

Justice Oliver Wendell Holmes wrote the opinion of the Court in which it agreed that Schenck had acted to undermine the draft. The Court decided that an individual act depended on the context, so while the flyers could have been considered harmless in peacetime, during war, they amounted to acts of national insubordination. This is where the famous analogy came about: The Court stated that if someone were to cry 'Fire!" in a park or at home, it would be one thing; to do so in a crowded theater would cause a panic and could not be justified by the principle of freedom of speech.

The ruling determined that while the First Amendment afforded generous rights when it came to free speech, there were limits to those rights, and context was what determined where those limits lay. The litmus test of those boundaries was whether the words would create a 'clear and present danger' that Congress had the right to prevent. Thus, the Court upheld Schenck's conviction.

Not only did this see Schenck go to jail for six months, it created a test that would be used by the Supreme Court to assess subsequent free speech challenges. However, this test only lasted for 50 years until *Brandenburg v Ohio* replaced it with the 'imminent lawless action' test, which protected a broader range of speech. The new test meant that the government could only limit speech inciting unlawful behavior for as long as it took for the police to arrive to prevent unlawful action.

Chapter 8

Brown v Board of Education, 1954

Where *Plessy v Ferguson* gave tacit permission for racial segregation, *Brown v Board of Education* was a landmark case that ended racial segregation, at least when it came to children in public schools. One of the most significant Supreme Court decisions of the 20th century, the landmark case did not end segregation in schools overnight, but it laid down in law that the Constitution upheld racial equality and gave impetus to the civil rights movement to step up its agitation for full racial equality.

In 1954, many parts of the southeastern United States had racially segregated schools, justified by the principles established in *Plessy v Ferguson*, which allowed for "separate but equal" facilities. However, there had been increasing calls by civil rights groups to challenge this, and in the early 1950s, NAACP lawyers brought a number of class-action lawsuits on behalf of black children and their families in Virginia, Delaware, South Carolina, and Kansas, looking to the courts to force school districts to allow black children to go to white public schools.

Representative-plaintiff Oliver Brown filed a class action against the Topeka, Kansas school board. A parent of a child who was not allowed to attend Topeka's white schools, he argued that Topeka's racial segregation violated the Constitution's Equal Protection Clause since the black and white schools were nowhere near equal to each other.

Initially, the federal district court dismissed his claim, determining that the schools were close enough to equal as to be constitutional, so Brown took his case to the Supreme Court, who reviewed all the school segregation actions at the same time.

Under the leadership of Chief Justice Earl Warren, the court decided that racial segregation in public schools was unconstitutional. The Equal Protection Clause of the Fourteenth Amendment prohibited any state from denying someone within its jurisdiction the full protection of the law. The Court took note of the fact that when Congress had drafted the Fourteenth Amendment in the 1860s, it had neither required nor prohibited integration in public schools. Regardless, the Fourteenth Amendment should be interpreted to guarantee an equal education in contemporary times. In the 20th century, public education was the foundation of democratic citizenship and professional training. If a state provided universal education, that education was a right and one which should be given equally to blacks and whites.

In order to determine whether the black and white schools really were equal, as the lower courts had decided, the Supreme Court carried out extensive research, including reviewing psychological studies. They concluded that since there was evidence to show that black girls in segregated schools had low self-esteem, segregation had a negative impact on black children's ability to learn. As a consequence, it did not matter whether facilities were equal. Racial segregation in and of itself was inherently unequal and therefore unconstitutional.

Plessy v Ferguson was overturned, at least as far as public schools were concerned. The following year, the Brown II case saw the Court order the states to integrate public schools "with all deliberate speed."

Not everyone was happy with the ruling. White resistance to the desegregation of schools saw violent clashes in some areas, with federal troops needing to be called in to Little Rock, Arkansas in 1957. Such resistance came to a head in 1958 with the case of *Cooper v Aaron*. The Court ruled that all states were constitutionally required to implement the Supreme Court's decision, regardless of personal feelings, forcing school boards to comply.

Racial integration across the south was finally achieved by the early 1970s. Meanwhile, the equal protection ruling in Brown covering schools spread to other areas of the law and out into the world of politics. Many historians agree that not only did *Brown v Board of Education* mark the dawn of the modern civil rights movement, but it was also a pivotal moment in the fight for racial equality in America.

Chapter 9

Miranda v Arizona, 1966

Miranda v Arizona gave rise to the 'Miranda rights' that anyone who has ever watched a cop show will be very familiar with. In this case, the Supreme Court ruled that anyone detained on suspicion of a crime should be told about their constitutional right to an attorney and against self-incrimination **before** police questioning could begin.

The case surrounded Phoenix resident Ernesto Miranda. In 1963, he was arrested and charged with rape, kidnapping, and robbery. The police interrogated him without telling him about his rights, and during the two-hour questioning, he was alleged to have confessed to the crimes, a confession the police recorded.

Miranda had failed to complete ninth grade and had a history of mental instability. He had no counsel, and thus the police could not be confident that the confession was legitimate.

Nevertheless, the prosecution relied solely on this confession to build their case and Miranda was found guilty of the rape and kidnapping and sentenced to 20-30 years in prison.

Miranda appealed to the Arizona Supreme Court, arguing that his confession was unconstitutionally acquired. The Court disagreed and his conviction stood. Miranda then appealed to the US Supreme Court, which reviewed the case.

The Supreme Court was divided, but in a 5-4 decision written by Chief Justice Earl Warren, finally ruled that Miranda's confession could not be used in evidence in a criminal trial because he had not been made aware of his rights. The Fifth Amendment obligated the police to warn suspects because it granted suspects the right to refuse to act as a witness against himself. In addition, the Sixth Amendment guaranteed all criminal defendants the right to an attorney.

The Court found that a defendant's right against self-incrimination had long been established in American law. Without that protection, the authorities were in a position to abuse their power, and the Court mentioned the use of police violence when obtaining confessions. The use of intimidation stripped suspects of their fundamental rights and could give rise to false confessions. Just as important was the right to an attorney, since their presence during an interrogation gives the defendant the support necessary to be able to tell their story "without fear." In the absence of these two rights, "no statement obtained from the defendant can truly be the product of his free choice."

Thus the 'Miranda Rights' were devised. The rights are a series of statements the police are obligated to tell someone who is being detained and interrogated. They include the right to remain silent and caution the defendant that anything they say can and will be used against them in a court of law. Further, the suspect needs to be told they have the right to an attorney and be provided with one to accompany them during interrogation if they cannot source one for themselves.

Since Ernesto Miranda was given none of these rights, his confession was unconstitutionally used at trial, and thus his conviction was quashed. However, it is worth noting that Miranda was subsequently retried and convicted without a confession.

Miranda v Arizona balanced the growing police powers with individual human rights. In establishing the Miranda Rights, it put in place a practice which remains essential today.

Chapter 10

Roe v Wade, 1973

In one of the Supreme Court's most controversial rulings to date, *Roe v Wade* determined that a state law banning abortions, except to save the life of the mother, was unconstitutional. The Court decided that the states: could not outlaw or regulate any aspect of abortions carried out during the first trimester of pregnancy; could only regulate abortions while making reasonable provisions for maternal health during the second trimester; and could only pass abortion laws protecting the life of the fetus in the third trimester and, even then, exceptions were to be made to protect the mother's life.

Roe v Wade caused a political uproar and divided the nation in a way few cases had ever done. While it might not be the most important decision the Supreme Court has ever made, most people have heard of *Roe v Wade* due to its far-reaching impact.

The sexual revolution and feminist movements of the 1960s had seen increasing demands for women's reproductive rights. At this time, most states either heavily restricted or banned outright abortions. In 1970, two recent law graduates, Linda Coffee and Sarah Weddington, brought a lawsuit against Henry Wade, Dallas County District Attorney, on behalf of Norma L McCorvey, aka Jane Roe, claiming that the Texan law criminalizing most abortions except where the mother's life was in danger was a violation of her constitutional rights. Roe was pregnant and held that, although her life was not in danger as a consequence of her pregnancy, she did not have the means to travel out of state and had the right to termination in a safe medical environment.

The Texas court ruled that the law was indeed a violation of the Constitution, so Wade appealed to the US Supreme Court.

The Court's decision was written by Justice Harry Blackmun, who had previously acted as counsel to the Mayo Clinic. The Court ruled 7-2 that the Texan law violated Jane Roe's constitutional right to privacy, as laid out in the First, Fourth, Ninth, and Fourteenth

Amendments, and referred to past cases which had found that marriage, contraception, and childrearing were activities which fell under this so-called 'zone of privacy.' The court found that this zone of privacy was broad enough to include a woman's right to choose whether or not to proceed with a pregnancy.

This ruling was important because it established that a woman's decision to terminate and how that termination was carried out where fundamental rights afforded constitutional protection, so any laws surrounding the matter must be deemed to be sufficiently 'important.'

Consequently, the Supreme Court examined whether the Texan law in question was suitably important to be constitutional. Looking at the history of abortion laws, delving as far back as ancient Greece, the Court found three justifications for banning abortions: A post-Victorian prejudice against 'illicit sexual conduct'; protecting women's health; protecting prenatal life. The Court felt that the first two justifications were irrelevant, given modern medical care and gender roles.

As far as the third justification was concerned, the Court found that prenatal life could not be held as falling under the definition of 'persons' as laid out in the US Constitution and that fetuses were only considered persons under criminal and civil law in very specific circumstances. Although culturally, some groups might recognize fetuses as people entitled to full rights, there was no universal consensus, so the Court ruled that the Texan law was elevating one view over many others. As a consequence, protecting all fetuses because of a controversial opinion meant that the law in question could not be deemed important enough to justify the banning of virtually all abortions.

This finding did not come without caveats. The Court did state that some state regulations around abortion could reach the threshold of being sufficiently important to qualify for being constitutional. For example, since a fetus might be viable in the third trimester due to advances in medical treatments, a state might decide to protect a fetus from third-trimester abortions except in cases where the mother's life was endangered. Similarly, since second- and third-trimester abortions carry an increased risk to the health of the mother, a state might choose to regulate abortions after three months' pregnancy to take this into account. However, the Court found that there was no issue 'important' enough to support regulation of first-trimester abortions, and these were solely for a patient and her doctor to decide.

Roe v Wade caused controversy when it was first released in January 1973, and it continues to be fiercely debated to this day. The case has been at the heart of many debates surrounding ethics, biology, and religion, and has been the definitive ruling for all these issues. Opponents on the Right side of the political spectrum argue that *Roe v Wade* allows for the ending of an innocent human life without genuinely constitutional justification. On the Left, critics claim that the reasoning behind the ruling was flawed and opened the door to a preventable backlash against women's reproductive rights.

Whatever individual opinion, the case demonstrates the power of the Court to impact on everyday individuals in a powerful, life-changing way.

Chapter 11

United States v Nixon, 1974

United States v Nixon put into practice one of the principles the Supreme Court had been founded on – that it had a duty to keep the other executive powers in check. The case resulted from the Watergate scandal, which had broken during the 1972 presidential campaign between Republican President Richard Nixon and Democrat Senator George McGovern.

On June 17, 1972, a few months before the election, five men broke into the Democratic National Committee headquarters in Washington DC. These men were subsequently found to be linked to the Nixon administration.

In May 1973, Attorney General Elliot Richardson appointed Archibald Cox as special prosecutor with the power to investigate the break-in. However, on October 20, Nixon ordered that Cox be fired, which led to what was dubbed the 'Saturday Night Massacre,' as Richardson and

Deputy Attorney General William Ruckelshaus both left their positions. There was an outcry over Cox's firing, leaving Nixon with no choice but to appoint Leon Jaworski as a replacement special prosecutor.

Jaworski got a subpoena in April 1974, which compelled Nixon to release tapes and papers connected to various meetings between the President and the suspects. It was believed that this would reveal damning evidence against the men and possibly even the President.

In an attempt to appease the special prosecutor, Nixon produced heavily edited transcripts of conversations required by the subpoena, hoping this would be enough to evade suspicion. His attorney then asked for the subpoena to be quashed. This request was denied, and the President was told to hand over unedited tapes and transcripts.

Nixon and Jaworski both appealed to the Supreme Court. Nixon's attorney stated that the matter was not one for judicial resolution, arguing that since it was an issue within the executive branch, it was down to the branch to deal with it. In addition, he stated that Jaworski had not sufficiently proven that the documents were essential for the case he was building against the suspects. Finally, he argued that Nixon enjoyed absolute executive privilege and thus had a right to protect any communications between high Government officials and their advisors and assistants.

It took less than three weeks for the Court to reach its decision, although there was never any significant doubt within the Court that it would find against the President. The question that needed to be decided was simply how to define what executive privilege was and what powers it conferred.

Multiple Justices had a hand in writing the judgment. The final draft featured Justice Blackmun's summary of the Facts of the Case, Justice Douglas's input on appeal, Justice Brennan's opinion on standing, Justice White's view of admissibility and relevance, and Justices Powell & Stewart's summation of executive privilege.

Such a broad range of inputs was reflective of the importance of the case. It was recognized that since the tapes Nixon was trying to bury probably held incontrovertible evidence of criminal wrongdoing by the President and his cohorts, so it was important there was no disagreement. Chief Justice Burger was responsible for delivering the decision from the bench, a decision that had been unanimous.

The Court determined that the Courts could indeed compel the President to release the material and that Jaworski had proven that it was likely that the tapes would contain information relevant to the charges under discussion. Although the Court acknowledged the principle of executive privilege, it stated that this did not mean that the President was above the law and could not claim total immunity from the judicial process no matter what the circumstance. In this instance, the Court found that Presidential privilege could not circumvent the judicial process in cases that did not reveal military or diplomatic secrets. Mere confidentiality was not sufficient reason to withhold evidence, and Nixon was ordered to hand over all unedited subpoenaed material to the District Court.

Sixteen days later, on August 9, 1974, Nixon resigned.

The case was important because it proved that the Court was not afraid of exerting its power over the highest of authorities if the situation merited it. Having been established as one of the checks and balances to keep federal power in its appropriate place, *United States v Nixon* demonstrated that the system worked.

Chapter 12

Obergefell v Hodges, 2015

Obergefell v Hodges saw the Supreme Court rule that the fundamental right to marry is guaranteed to same-sex couples under the Fourteenth Amendment. The decision was close, with the Associate Justices ruling 5-4 in favor of requiring all states to perform and recognize same-sex marriages as having the same legal standing as opposite-sex couple marriages.

Between January 2012 and February 2014, plaintiffs in Kentucky, Michigan, Ohio, and Tennessee filed a number of federal district court cases which led to Obergefell v Hodges. All the district courts found in favor of the plaintiffs, and the rulings were appealed to the Sixth Circuit. Following a series of appeals in the Fourth, Seventh, Ninth, and Tenth Circuits, the case was handed to the Supreme Court for review.

Having consolidated the four same-sex marriage cases into one (*Obergefell v Hodges*), the Court decided to order briefing and oral argument on just two questions: Did the Fourteenth Amendment compel a state to license a same-sex marriage; and did the Fourteenth Amendment mean that a state had to recognize a same-sex marriage? In addition, the parties to the individual cases were instructed to consider only the question(s) pertaining to their specific case.

Obergefell v Hodges had almost 150 amici curiae briefs, more than any other Supreme Court case. Amicus curiae are people who are not directly involved in a case who are there to support the court by giving information, knowledge, or insight which impact on the issues raised. The briefs included one written by Morgan Lewis' partner, Susan Baker Manning, on behalf of almost 400 business entities which laid out a business argument for legalizing same-sex marriage.

When the Court delivered its verdict, it overruled the previous decision made in *Baker v Nelson* which had been used as precedent by the Sixth Circuit. However, the four Justices who had been outvoted issued dissenting opinions, with Chief Justice Roberts reading out part of his opinion from the bench, a first since he had been appointed to the Court in 2005.

Nevertheless, the Court decided that state same-sex marriage bans were a violation of the Fourteenth Amendment's Due Process and Equal Protection Clauses. It argued that the Constitution granted liberty to all, which included the right of an individual to lawfully define and express their identity. Cases such as *Zablocki v Redhail* and *Loving v Virginia* had established a fundamental right to marry, and the Court found four main reasons why this right should be extended to same-sex couples: First, the right to choose to marry (or not) is inherently bound to the concept of individual autonomy. Second, the right to marry is a fundamental right because it allows the union of two people, which is unlike any other in terms of importance to the individuals concerned. Third, the fundamental right to marry protects children and families, conferring rights of childrearing, procreation, and education. Since same-sex couples have children and families, this safeguard should be extended to them, although the Court noted that in the United States, the right to marry was never conditional on procreation. Fourth, the Court stated that since 'marriage is a keystone of our social order,' banning same-sex couples from marriage meant that they were denied the many benefits of marriage, bringing a level of instability to their relationships with no just cause.

The Court considered the Due Process and Equal Protection Clauses and found that same-sex marriage bans ran contra to the latter. As such, the Court eliminated same-sex marriage bans and upheld the notion that same-sex couples had the fundamental right to marry in all fifty states and enjoy the same rights and responsibilities as opposite-sex couples. Further, all states were ordered to recognize same-sex marriages that had been legally carried out in other states.

The White House was lit up with rainbow colors on the night of the Supreme Court's ruling, with then-President Barack Obama describing the decision as a 'victory for America.' James Obergefell, who had started legal proceedings so that his name could be listed on his husband's death certificate as the surviving spouse, said, "Today's ruling from the Supreme Court affirms what millions across the country already know to be true in our hearts: that our love is equal."

Not everyone was happy with the outcome. For example, Texas Attorney General Ken Paxton called the outcome a "lawless ruling" and offered free legal support to state workers who did not want to marry couples due to their religious beliefs. Some Christian organizations expressed a fear that the Court's decision conflicted with the principle of religious liberty, an argument that had been presented by the dissenting judges.

Despite the ruling, there are still some counties in Alabama and Texas that do not issue marriage licenses to same-sex couples, and same-sex couples living in those counties must travel elsewhere to marry. However, even then, there can be complications, since some counties require at least one person in a couple to be a resident of that county to obtain a marriage license.

Obergefell v. Hodges was seen as a victory for same-sex couples and their families, and it may well be the springboard for the recognition of additional rights for other marginalized groups.

Conclusion

Since its inception, the Supreme Court of the United States has striven to act as a bastion of American values, regardless of the prevailing political tides. This book has reviewed some of the most important and influential cases presided over by the court, but there have been countless more, all influencing American society, culture, and laws. When necessary, the Court has upheld the law against some of the most powerful people and institutions, ensuring that a balance is maintained between the various political houses and organizations.

Recently, the Supreme Court suffered the loss of Ruth Bader Ginsburg. Affectionately known as RBG, Ginsburg died at the age of 87 following a battle with pancreatic cancer. Ginsburg had a record of championing gender equality and social justice throughout her career, even before her appointment to the Supreme Court in 1993. President Trump described her as a "legal giant and pioneer for women" who would inspire Americans "for generations to come."

Reportedly, Ginsburg's dying wish was that she would not be replaced until after the US election in November 2020, and some have argued that there is precedent for her wish to be respected.

In March 2016, then-President Barack Obama nominated Merrick Garland for Associate Justice of the US Supreme Court, following the death of Antonin Scalia. However, before Obama announced his nomination, Senate Majority Leader Mitch McConnell stated that the sitting president should not be allowed to appoint a Supreme Court Justice since it should be chosen by the next president, who would be elected later that year. His statement caused outrage among Senate Democrats, who argued that there was more than enough time to vote on a nominee before the election.

It was the first time in over a century that a Democratic president had the chance to nominate a Supreme Court justice while the Republicans were in control of the Senate, a situation which had last occurred in 1895. Previously, a Democratic-led Senate had confirmed Republican President Reagan's nomination of Anthony Kennedy in 1988, and in 1991, a narrow Democratic majority still accepted the appointment of Justice Clarence Thomas.

At the time of his death, Scalia was viewed as being one of the most conservative members of the Court, so although Garland was broadly politically neutral, any appointment less conservative than Scalia held the potential to change the ideological approach of the Court for years to come, since, once appointed to the Supreme Court, an individual holds the position for life. Had Garland been appointed, liberal Justices would have been in the majority for the first time since the confirmation of Harry Blackmun in 1970.

However, the Senate Judiciary Committee's Republican majority decided against holding the necessary hearings to advance the vote to the Senate at large, leaving Garland's nomination to expire in January 2017. This was the first time since the Civil War that a nominee whose nomination was not withdrawn was not considered for a vacant position in the Court, and when Donald Trump assumed the Presidency, he nominated Judge Neil Gorsuch for the vacancy, assuring a continued conservative slant.

Although the Republicans blocked Obama's nomination, arguing that it was too close to an election, this has not prevented Trump nominating Amy Coney Barrett to replace Ruth Bader Ginsburg. He described Barrett as "a woman of unparalleled achievement, towering intellect, sterling credentials, and unyielding loyalty to the constitution" and asked Senate Republicans to confirm his nominee before the November election. If this occurs, the Supreme Court will be made up of a 6-3 conservative majority. While this might rankle those who feel that the Republicans should respect their own argument and not appoint a new Supreme Court Justice until after the election, the reality is that the Democrats have little power to prevent Barrett's confirmation.

In fact, there is only one possibility, according to scholars. If the Republicans were to agree not to push through Trump's nominee, the Democrats would agree not to increase the number of Supreme Court justices on the bench, something they have threatened to do if their candidate wins the White House and they win the back control of the Senate.

If this happened, it would not be the first time an attempt would be made to change the makeup of the Supreme Court for political purposes. In the late 1930s, President Franklin D Roosevelt tried to introduce the 'court-packing plan.' He aimed to place limits on the court when it came to the age of justices. Since a justice held their position until death, Roosevelt proposed that up to six additional justices could be appointed for every existing justice who was older than 70 years and six months, and who had served for ten years or more. Largely viewed as a political move to fill the Court with his supporters so he could get favorable rulings on New Deal legislation, Roosevelt's Judicial Procedures Reform Bill of 1937 was never even voted on in Congress. The justices immediately went public with their opposition to the plan, countering Roosevelt's argument that they needed help with their workload with the fact that they were fully up to date. The public was not in favor either, and Roosevelt was forced to drop the idea and revert to doing what every other President had done – influence the Court with appointments when vacancies came up.

Just as in Roosevelt's time, the chances of a deal preventing Barrett's confirmation are slim. With the Republicans holding a majority in the Senate, there is little incentive to agree to such a proposal. While the Democrats could try to delay

Barrett's confirmation, it is unlikely they can stop it completely. With the Republicans holding a 53-47 majority in the Senate chamber, they have the numbers to confirm Barrett's appointment.

Whoever is appointed RBG's successor, one thing is for sure: The Supreme Court will continue to review cases and uphold the constitution in the way it deems most appropriate.

Made in the USA
Middletown, DE
18 October 2020